PIANO / VOCAL / GUIT

P9-CQP-966

TOP HITS OF 2015

ISBN 978-1-4950-3543-2

HAL•LEONARD® CORPORATION
7777 W. BLUEMOUND RD. P.O. BOX 13819 MILWAUKEE, WI 53213

Visit Hal Leonard Online at
www.halleonard.com

CONTENTS

BLANK SPACE

Words and Music by TAYLOR SWIFT,
MAX MARTIN and SHELLBACK

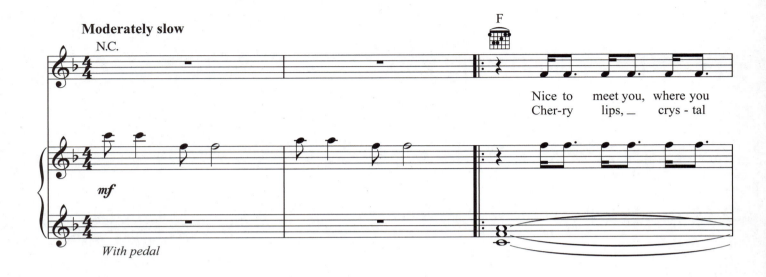

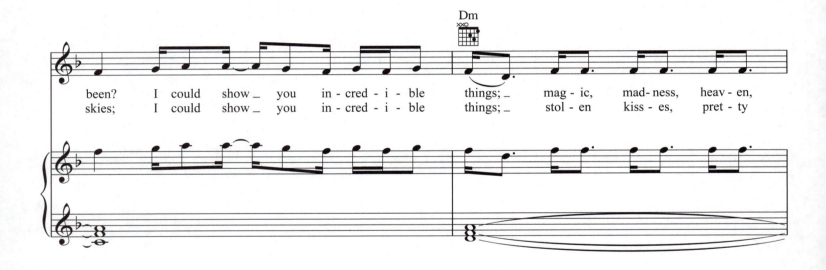

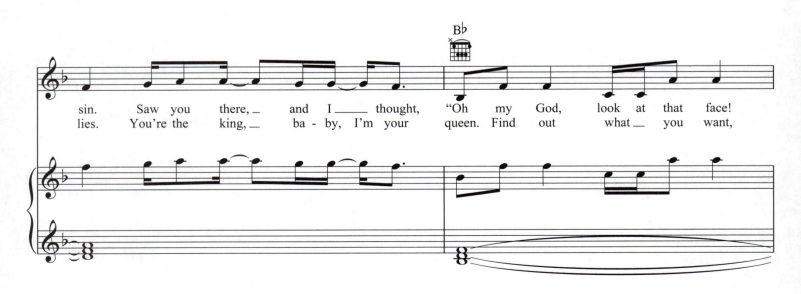

Boys on-ly want love if it's tor - ture. Don't say I did-n't,

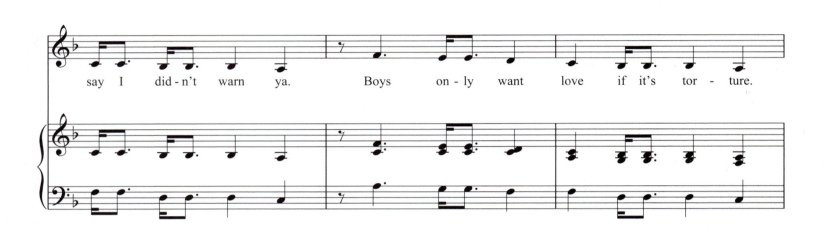

say I did-n't warn ya. Boys on-ly want love if it's tor - ture.

D.S. al Coda

Don't say I did-n't, say I did-n't warn ya.

CODA

- by, and I'll write your name. ___

BUDAPEST

Words and Music by GEORGE BARNETT
and JOEL POTT

Ba - by, if you hold me then all ____ of this will go ____ a - way. ___

To Coda

D.S. al Coda
(take 2nd ending)

CHEERLEADER

Words and Music by OMAR PASLEY,
MARK BRADFORD, CLIFTON DILLON,
SLY DUNBAR and RYAN DILLON

When I need mo-ti-va-tion,
walks like a mod-el;

my one so-lu-tion is my queen, __ 'cause she stay strong, __
she grants my wish-es like a ge-nie in a bot-tle, ____

EARNED IT
(Fifty Shades of Grey)
from FIFTY SHADES OF GREY

Words and Music by ABEL TESFAYE,
AHMAD BALSHE, STEPHAN MOCCIO
and JASON QUENNEVILLE

work it, the way you work it. 'Cause, girl, you earned, _____ earned, ___

earned, _____ earned, __ earned, _____ earned __ it. _____

Lead vocal ad lib. until end

HEARTBEAT SONG

Words and Music by JASON EVIGAN,
MITCH ALLAN, KARA DioGUARDI
and AUDRA MAE

Moderately fast

This is my heart - beat song _ and I'm _ gon-na play _ it. Been _ so long, _ I for-got _

_ how to turn _ it up, _ up, up, _ up all _ night long, _ oh, up, _ up all _ night long. _

You, where the hell did you come from? _

* Recorded a half step lower.

I LIVED

Words and Music by RYAN TEDDER
and NOEL ZANCANELLA

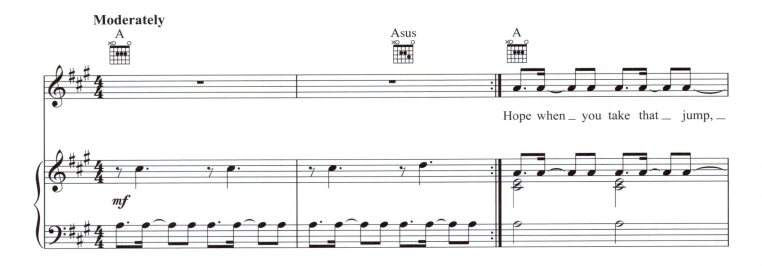

I REALLY LIKE YOU

Words and Music by CARLY RAE JEPSEN,
PETER SVENSSON and JACOB KASHER HINDLIN

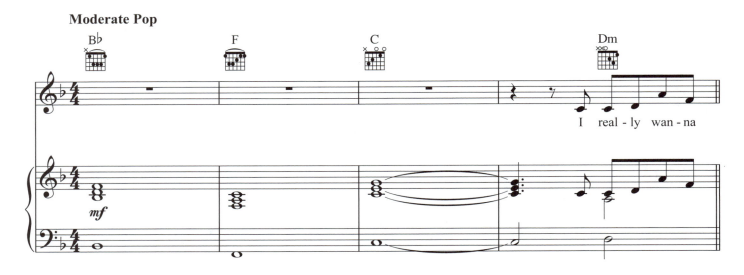

Moderate Pop

I real-ly wan-na

stop, but I just got the taste for it. I feel like I could fly with the boy on the moon._
say is a sweet rev-e-la-a-tion. All I wan-na do is get in-to your head._

So, hon-ey, hold my hand, you like mak-in' me wait for it. I feel like I could
Yeah, we could stay a-lone, you and me and this temp-ta-tion, sip-pin' on your

LOVE ME LIKE YOU DO

from FIFTY SHADES OF GREY

Words and Music by MAX MARTIN,
SAVAN KOTECHA, ILYA,
ALI PAYAMI and TOVE LO

LAY ME DOWN

Words and Music by SAM SMITH,
JAMES NAPIER and ELVIN SMITH

Poco rubato (♩ = 50)

Yes, I do, I be-lieve. That one day I will be where I was right there, right next to you.___

___ And it's hard, the days just seem so dark. The moon, the stars are noth-ing with-out you. Your

touch, your skin, where do I be-gin? No words can ex-plain the way I'm miss-ing you.___

LIPS ARE MOVIN

Words and Music by KEVIN KADISH
and MEGHAN TRAINOR

Bright Dance beat

You on-ly love me when you're_ here._ You're so _____ two-faced, two-faced, babe,_

D.S. al Coda

_____ ooh. _ You can buy _

CODA

I know you lie, 'cause your lips are
lyin', lyin', lyin', ba - by.)

mov - ing. Tell _ me, do you think I'm _ dumb? _____ I might be

young, but I ain't stu - pid, talk - in' 'round in cir - cles _ with

Additional Lyrics

Rap: Boy, look at me in my face!
Tell me that you're not just about this bass.
You really think I could be replaced?
Nah, I come from outer space!
And I'm a classy girl, I'm-a hold it up.
You're full of something, but it ain't love.
And what we got, straight overdue.
Go find somebody new.

MASTERPIECE

Words and Music by BRITTANY BURTON,
JOSHUA BERMAN and EMILY SCHWARTZ

So much pres- sure: why so loud? If you don't like my sound, you can turn it down. I got a road, and I walk it a - lone.

Eb

mas - ter - piece, and I... (Oh, _____ oh, _____ oh, _____

To Coda ⊕

Cm **Fm** **Ab**

ah.) _____ (Oh, _____ oh, _____ oh, _____

1 **2** **Eb**

ah.) _____ Those who ah.) _____ I still fall on my

Fm7 **Bb** **Cm**

face some - times, __ and I can't col - or in - side the lines, __ 'cause

ONE LAST TIME

Words and Music by SAVAN KOTECHA,
DAVID GUETTA, GIORGIO TUINFORT,
CARL FALK and RAMI YACOUB

SEE YOU AGAIN
from FURIOUS 7

Words and Music by CAMERON THOMAZ,
CHARLIE PUTH, JUSTIN FRANKS
and ANDREW CEDAR

It's been a long day __ with-out you, my friend. _ And I'll

tell you all a-bout it when I see you a-gain. _ We've come a long way __ from

where we be-gan. __ Oh, I'll tell you all a-bout it when I see you a-gain, when I

POCKET FULL OF DREAMS

Words and Music by BRITTANY CARLSON,
JACOB HOGGARD and RUNE WESTBERG

SHUT UP AND DANCE

Words and Music by RYAN McMAHON,
BEN BERGER, SEAN WAUGAMAN,
ELI MAIMAN, NICHOLAS PETRICCA
and KEVIN RAY

Recorded a half step lower.

STYLE

Words and Music by TAYLOR SWIFT,
MAX MARTIN, SHELLBACK and ALI PAYAMI

Moderate Pop feel

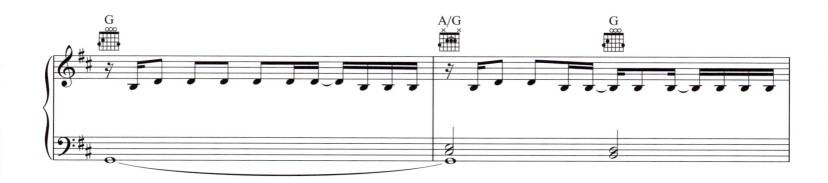

THINKING OUT LOUD

Words and Music by ED SHEERAN
and AMY WADGE

SUGAR

Words and Music by ADAM LEVINE,
HENRY WALTER, JOSHUA COLEMAN,
LUKASZ GOTTWALD, JACOB KASHER HINDLIN
and MIKE POSNER

*Recorded a half step lower.

WANT TO WANT ME

Words and Music by JASON DESROULEAUX,
MITCH ALLAN, LINDY ROBBINS,
SAM MARTIN and IAN KIRKPATRICK

Moderate Dance groove

foot out the door. Where are my keys? ___ 'Cause I got-ta leave, ___

___ yeah. ___ In the back of the cab, ___ I tip the wear-ing

driv-er a-head of time. "Get me there fast." ___ I got your
noth-ing ___ but a smile. Fell to the floor, ___ and you

bod-y on my mind, I want it bad. ___ Ooh, just the
whis-per in my ear, "Ba-by, I'm yours." ___ Ooh, just the

thought of you gets me so high, so high.

thought of you gets me so high, so high.

Girl, you're the one I want to want me. And if you want

me, girl, you got me. There's noth-ing I know I would-n't

do, (I would-n't do) just to get up next to you.

UPTOWN FUNK

Words and Music by MARK RONSON,
BRUNO MARS, PHILIP LAWRENCE,
JEFF BHASKER, DEVON GALLASPY,
NICHOLAUS WILLIAMS, LONNIE SIMMONS,
RONNIE WILSON, CHARLES WILSON,
RUDOLPH TAYLOR and ROBERT WILSON

THE NEW DECADE SERIES

THE BEST EVER COLLECTION
ARRANGED FOR PIANO, VOICE AND GUITAR

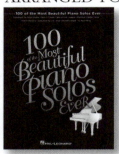

100 of the Most Beautiful Piano Solos Ever
100 songs
00102787 ....$27.50

150 of the Most Beautiful Songs Ever
150 ballads
00360735 ....$27.00

150 More of the Most Beautiful Songs Ever
150 songs
00311318 ....$29.99

More of the Best Acoustic Rock Songs Ever
69 tunes
00311738 ....$19.95

Best Acoustic Rock Songs Ever
65 acoustic hits
00310984 ....$19.95

Best Big Band Songs Ever
68 big band hits
00359129 ....$17.99

Best Blues Songs Ever
73 blues tunes
00312874 ....$19.99

Best Broadway Songs Ever
83 songs
00309155 ....$24.99

More of the Best Broadway Songs Ever
82 songs
00311501 ....$22.95

Best Children's Songs Ever
102 songs
00310358 ....$22.99

Best Christmas Songs Ever
69 holiday favorites
00359130 ....$24.99

Best Classic Rock Songs Ever
64 hits
00310800 ....$22.99

Best Classical Music Ever
86 classical favorites
00310674 (Piano Solo) $19.95

The Best Country Rock Songs Ever
52 hits
00118881 ....$19.99

Best Country Songs Ever
78 classic country hits
00359135 ....$19.99

Best Disco Songs Ever
50 songs
00312565 ....$19.99

Best Dixieland Songs Ever
90 songs
00312326 ....$19.99

Best Early Rock 'n' Roll Songs Ever
74 songs
00310816 ....$19.95

Best Easy Listening Songs Ever
75 mellow favorites
00359193 ....$19.99

Best Folk/Pop Songs Ever
66 hits
00138299 ....$19.99

Best Gospel Songs Ever
80 gospel songs
00310503 ....$19.99

Best Hymns Ever
118 hymns
00310774 ....$18.99

Best Jazz Piano Solos Ever
80 songs
00312079 ....$19.99

Best Jazz Standards Ever
77 jazz hits
00311641 ....$19.95

More of the Best Jazz Standards Ever
74 beloved jazz hits
00311023 ....$19.95

Best Latin Songs Ever
67 songs
00310355 ....$19.99

Best Love Songs Ever
62 favorite love songs
00359198 ....$19.99

Best Movie Songs Ever
71 songs
00310063 ....$19.99

Best Pop/Rock Songs Ever
50 classics
00138279 ....$19.99

Best Praise & Worship Songs Ever
80 all-time favorites
00311057 ....$22.99

More of the Best Praise & Worship Songs Ever
76 songs
00311800 ....$24.99

Best R&B Songs Ever
66 songs
00310184 ....$19.95

Best Rock Songs Ever
63 songs
00490424 ....$18.95

Best Showtunes Ever
71 songs
00118782 ....$19.99

Best Songs Ever
72 must-own classics
00359224 ....$24.99

Best Soul Songs Ever
70 hits
00311427 ....$19.95

Best Standards Ever, Vol. 1 (A-L)
72 beautiful ballads
00359231 ....$17.95

Best Standards Ever, Vol. 2 (M-Z)
73 songs
00359232 ....$17.99

More of the Best Standards Ever, Vol. 1 (A-L)
76 all-time favorites
00310813 ....$17.95

More of the Best Standards Ever, Vol. 2 (M-Z)
75 stunning standards
00310814 ....$17.95

Best Torch Songs Ever
70 sad and sultry favorites
00311027 ....$19.95

Best Wedding Songs Ever
70 songs
00311096 ....$19.95

Prices, contents and availability subject to change without notice. Not all products available outside the U.S.A.

Visit us online for complete songlists at
www.halleonard.com

0615